The Bread
of Life

The Bread of Life

A Guide to the Lord's Supper for Presbyterians

RONALD P. BYARS

Geneva Press
Louisville, Kentucky

© 2005 Ronald P. Byars

Scripture quotations from the New Revised Standard Version of the Bible are copyright © 1989 by the Division of Christian Education of the National Council of the Churches of Christ in the U.S.A. and are used by permission.

Excerpts from *Book of Common Worship*, © 1993 Westminster John Knox Press.

Excerpts from "Festival Canticle," *Lutheran Book of Worship*, text © 1978 Lutheran Book of Worship. Used by permission of Augsburg Fortress.

Book design by Sharon Adams
Cover design by Teri Vinson

First edition
Published by Geneva Press
Louisville, Kentucky

This book is printed on acid-free paper that meets the American National Standards Institute Z39.48 standard. ♾

PRINTED IN THE UNITED STATES OF AMERICA

05 06 07 08 09 10 11 12 13 14 — 10 9 8 7 6 5 4 3 2 1

Library of Congress Cataloging-in-Publication Data
Byars, Ronald P.
    The bread of life : a guide to the Lord's Supper for Presbyterians / Ronald Byars.—1st ed.
        p. cm.
    ISBN 0-664-50258-X (alk. paper)
    1. Lord's Supper—Presbyterian Church. I. Title.

BX9189.C5B93 2004
264'.051036—dc22   2004052303

This little book is dedicated
to all those whose
study and labor
led to the creation of the
Book of Common Worship, *1993*

Contents

INTRODUCTION

When the presiding minister invites the congregation to the Lord's Table, she or he may use these words from the *Book of Common Worship:* "Friends, this is the joyful feast of the people of God!" I can imagine that these words may come as a shock to some: "joyful"? "feast"?

For many of us, the Lord's Supper seems far distant from anything having to do with a feast or with joy. The Supper has often felt as though it were a kind of replay of the *Last* Supper, which Jesus shared with his disciples on the night when he was betrayed. Understood in those terms, it feels more like a very sober, even mournful, introspective occasion, as though it's meant to lead us back to a time *before* the resurrection of the Lord. However, for us, there is no such thing as Christ crucified and *not* risen. From earliest centuries, Christians assembled on the day of the Lord's resurrection (Sunday) to gather at the Table to meet the Lord who is *both* crucified and risen. Those early celebrations were just that— joyful feasts, in which the gathered congregation sensed that they were eating and drinking with the risen Christ.

In the past few decades, both Protestants and Roman Catholics have begun to rediscover the feast as true celebration, an outpouring of thanksgiving for God's work of redemption in Christ and joyful gratitude for the promise that God will surely finish what has been begun in Christ. As Presbyterians and others have revised our rites, we have found ancient models useful in helping us to recover a "joyful feast." The Lord's Supper is rooted in the past, but it's not about the past. Rather, it turns our eyes toward God's promised future.

What does it take to transform our Communion services in ways that make them clearly joyful? The words of the rite as provided or described in denominational sources may help. But the Lord's Supper is not just about words. Even if the minister should say, "Friends, this is the joyful feast of the people of God," the words may not be enough to overcome other signals that say just the opposite.

In two congregations I have been privileged to serve, we groped our way toward a "joyful feast," and one of the ways we did that was to celebrate the Lord's Supper every Sunday. It was necessary to think through the celebration with care. Not only was it important to think about what words we would use as we prayed at the Table, but also, what song? What movement, what gesture might signal "joyful feast"? I am deeply grateful to Second Presbyterian Church, Lexington, Kentucky; and to First Presbyterian Church, Birmingham, Michigan, for the many joyful feasts I was privileged to share with them. I hope that this little book may open the door for others who will learn both to expect and to experience the Lord's Supper, Holy Communion, the Eucharist as a "joyful feast of the people of God."

CHAPTER 1

WHAT'S EATING
AND DRINKING
GOT TO DO WITH FAITH?

Imagine having wandered into a Sunday church
service if you had never gone to church before.
You might be visiting friends for the weekend.
They have a child in the children's choir, so what
could you do but go along? Or a fellow band
member from your school is playing in a brass
quartet for the eleven o'clock service, and two or
three of you have come to offer support. Or perhaps you are simply curious; or, more than curious, you have felt yourself pulled into some sort
of spiritual search and, for reasons not clear even
to you, landed in this Presbyterian congregation,
having chosen a seat nearest the exit.

Much of what you see and hear is relatively
familiar from experiences you have had with
other kinds of public assembly. The whole congregation sings together, the way the crowd sings
"The Star-spangled Banner" at the opening of

the ball game. Someone stands up to speak, not unlike a dozen other occasions from high school commencement to a sales meeting, class, or political rally. Other sights and sounds are unfamiliar. The strangest of all is the praying and singing over a little bit of food on the table that stands in front of the congregation. After the praying and singing, women and men distribute tiny portions of bread and wine to the people. There is hardly enough to satisfy an appetite or quench a thirst. What can this be about?

Maybe there is no one in your community for whom the church's celebration of Holy Communion would be unfamiliar, but the statistical probabilities that there will be such persons are growing exponentially. More and more people in North American society have never been exposed to the ritual action of the Lord's Supper in a Christian church. If one of them were to ask you the meaning of this rite, what would you answer? To say that the bread represents Christ's body, and the wine represents his blood, would be true, but at the same time it would likely make no sense to someone who doesn't know the language and the stories of the Bible and church.

For that matter, many folks who are already members of churches may wonder what this bread and wine ritual is all about, even though they know the conventional explanations. Why do we need a ritual, anyway? J. J. von Allmen, a Swiss

Reformed minister and scholar, has charged that since the dawn of the modern era Protestantism "has never known quite what to do about the sacraments and . . . is challenged more strongly by the sacraments than by anything else."

Around 1832, Ralph Waldo Emerson, pastor of a Unitarian congregation, asked the church officers to discontinue the use of the Lord's Supper. His argument was that symbolic actions might have been appropriate to people in the ancient Middle East, but they were "foreign and unsuited" to us. The church officers declined to accept Emerson's recommendation; nevertheless, Emerson had said out loud what a lot of people thought, and what many others in our own time think, even if they don't say it. North Americans, by and large, are a people for whom ritual actions seem alien and artificial. We are inclined to be suspicious of them, as though they are nothing more than a poor substitute for what might better be simply and clearly explained. We prefer ideas to symbolic actions.

Except. Except when the neighbor's daughter vanished, and everyone spontaneously began tying yellow ribbons around the trees. Except when a classmate's car crossed the median and killed him and three members of our class, and we all drove out to the crash site and left flowers and teddy bears and notes on the spot where the car had come to rest. Except when, at the end of a fabulous concert, we all lighted matches or lighters or candles and held them up high while we swayed and sang along with the band. Except when we installed new members of our fraternity, or initiated new members of our club. Except at almost every wedding in our church, when the bride's first choice is for her father to escort her down the aisle to the waiting arm of her groom, even though she does not for a minute believe that she is being transferred from the custody of one man to the custody of another.

In fact, we Americans are good at inventing rituals with flowers, candles, stuffed animals, ribbons, poetry, handclasps, and special songs. Somehow, when intense feelings are involved, words don't seem to be enough. No one ever asks what use our deceased classmate might have for the teddy bear left on her lawn. No one ever requires an explanation for why we painted our faces green and white when Michigan State made it to the Final Four. Ritual is intuitive. It makes sense when words don't make sense, or when making sense isn't enough.

Do you suppose it's possible that, when it comes to church, we've learned to reduce faith to believing in a doctrine, or learning certain rules of behavior? If that's all it's about, then sermons certainly make sense, but ritual actions would seem to remove us one or two degrees from the lucid explanations that serve so well in understanding doctrine and ethics. But what if faith, as Christians experience it, is more than believing and doing certain things? What if faith is, first of all, relationship? And what if our assembly for worship is about cultivating that relationship? a relationship between God and a people? between persons and other persons with whom they are united in Christ?

A little bit of bread, a tiny sip from the cup, will certainly not serve as adequate nourishment for the body. However, a little bread and a little wine send signals to the deep layers of our unconscious. When the bread comes from a hearty loaf, the aroma triggers our memories of fresh bread eaten at the table with loved ones all around. As we enter the sanctuary, we can smell the wine, and for many it evokes memories of conviviality. The psalmist knew similar experiences, and praised God for having given "wine to gladden the human heart . . . and bread to strengthen the human heart" (Ps. 104:15).

Sight and smell and taste combine to stir around in the emotional depths rooted in our experience. The sight, smell, and taste of fresh bread may not make us think of actual occasions we experienced in our birth family, but may nevertheless evoke the sorts of feelings that people learn at a table surrounded by familiar and beloved faces. Or maybe it was some other table—a table of hospitality far from home, or the "table"

shared with others in a wilderness camp, or the
table of the cafeteria when we were in first grade
or when we were away from home at school. Most
likely, the loaf will evoke all those experiences,
undifferentiated, mixed together. Bread is more
than it may seem when we're thinking about it in
practical terms as we put together our lunch for
tomorrow. Bread is relief from hunger, it's satis-
faction, and it's acceptance and laughter and
home. Wine is celebrations, time out from the
burdens of work, the delight of friendships new
and old. (More often, in Presbyterian congregations, the "wine" is grape juice. But even grape
juice has about it something of the aroma of the
same grape that, given time, becomes wine.)

Perhaps one of the reasons that we people in
Western societies so often find ourselves puzzled
or put off by sacramental rituals is that we have
inherited a cultural suspicion of the material
world. That may be hard to believe, since we live
in a society that seems to be accurately described
as materialistic. The slick-paper magazines lure us
with food and drink and leather and fine fabrics to
wear or hang on the walls. We revel in the material substance of the world! But, at the same time,
we divide the material world from the spiritual.
When we go in search of "spirituality," more
often than not we are looking for something invis-
ible and intangible. To achieve a spiritual state, we
imagine that we have to close our eyes, to medi-

tate, to withdraw from the sensory world that surrounds us. In church, being spiritual seems to mean quietly exploring one's own heart and mind.

This division between "spiritual" and "material," as though the two are profoundly incompatible, is a curious phenomenon that's peculiar to European and American society, and not shared by most other societies in the world (until they feel the impact of our influence). In fact, this division was not characteristic even of our European forebears until, perhaps, the beginning of the seventeenth century. This separation of spiritual from material was unknown to the peoples of the Bible, and is not rooted in either Jewish or Christian theology. In fact, the foundation of Christian theology is the doctrine of the incarnation—the affirmation that, in Christ, God became a human being. Specifically, God drew near to us in the person of Jesus of Nazareth.

The doctrine of the incarnation says that God does not despise the material world, but has, in fact, become flesh and blood for our sakes. The material world is hallowed—made holy—by the incarnation. If human beings know God at all, it is only because of God's own action. God moved toward us in Christ, and that movement was into the same material world that frames our existence. We cannot step out of the material world to know God outside of it. "And the Word became flesh and lived among us, and we have seen his glory, the glory as of a father's only son, full of grace and truth" (John 1:14).

Because the church believes that God has become incarnate in Christ in an act of self-revelation, we are not embarrassed by the material world, nor do we aspire to shake it off. We use real rather than imaginary water when we baptize, and when we celebrate the Lord's Supper we use real food. Water, bread, and wine derive from the world God has created and in which God has come to us. The Spirit becomes manifest in the use of ordinary everyday things set apart by prayer to a special use.

There is not a society in the world that is indifferent to the emotional and cultural significance of meals. Not every society is accustomed to the uses of wheat flour, or of the juice of the grape, fermented or unfermented. Still, every society has its choice staple food and its convivial drink. Nor has it been uncommon in various societies for a meal of some sort to be associated with religious faith and religious rites. Food equates with life, after all. Eating and drinking, we take into our own bodies the fruits of the earth that sustain life. It is this nourishment that enables physical growth, thought, and action. It has often been said that we are what we eat. In the Lord's Supper, we understand Jesus Christ to be our nourishment— our food and drink. He is bread to strengthen the human heart, and wine to make it glad.

But wait a minute! What sense does it make to say that Jesus is bread, or that he is wine? Most of us hear those figures of speech and make the appropriate associations without having to have them explained. Clearly, Jesus is not bread, not wine. To say that A is B, as in "Jesus is bread," is to use a device that language teachers call metaphor. Metaphors are themselves symbols made of words. The symbols say what is not so easily or profoundly said in lengthy explanations. For example, we say that our good friend is a rock, meaning not that she is made of some hard substance, but that she is utterly dependable in a crisis. Or we say that the attorney we've hired to represent our case is a tiger, meaning not that he is a wild animal, but that he's a fierce advocate for those he supports. In our hymns, we say that God is a "mighty fortress," or a "shepherd." If we were to use only a single metaphor for God, and never any other, we would be saying too little about God, or too much, and the result would be a distortion. When we set one metaphor next to another, it works. We begin to see how, all together, they begin to yield for us a picture of God that's layered with images, thoughts, and feelings. Jesus, then, is good shepherd, living water, our way, our truth, our resurrection, our life. And Jesus is bread and wine—food for the soul.

The Lord's Supper itself is a metaphor made tangible in bread, wine, and prayer. We can smell it, touch it, taste it, and hear it, and it says, over and over, speaking to every level of our conscious or unconscious minds: Jesus is bread and wine— for us, and for everyone whose spirit is hungry and thirsty. The ritual of the Lord's Supper is not an expendable symbol that we can abandon once we have mastered the ideas and doctrines represented in its celebration. The rite is as necessary as— more necessary than—multiple explanations of it. We eat and drink, before God, what we can know and experience only with our whole body and soul, all five senses engaged.

Some Questions for Thought

Can you identify occasions in your life that called for some sort of "ritual"—some gesture or symbolic action that said something that words couldn't quite manage?

Do you remember times of laughter, storytelling, or just quiet solidarity with others sitting around some sort of table where you had shared a meal?

What material things in your own home or workplace speak to your heart and head about absent loved ones or beloved places or cherished experiences?

What images come to your mind when you think about bread? wine?

CHAPTER 2

LOOKING BACKWARD: WE'VE BEEN THIS WAY BEFORE

Ritual is a kind of playfulness. If you imagine that playfulness is the opposite of serious-ness, just watch how children play. Children's play may be filled with silliness and laughter, but it can also be quite sober and earnest. At the Children's Museum, my five-year-old grandson loves to try on all the roles available in the miniature supermarket, with its plastic fruits, meats, and vegetables, its shopping baskets, its cash registers. His play is his work, undertaken with dedication as well as delight. A grand-daughter's pretend tea party is a serious busi-ness, with each step taken in its proper order. No sipping before pouring! Children's playful-ness may serve a number of purposes, but one purpose is surely to see what it feels like to be Dad or Mom, a tiger in the jungle, or a fire-fighter coming to the rescue.

Adults don't outgrow the need for playfulness. They simply substitute grownup kinds of playfulness for the child's. At the high school commencement, budding adults don cap and gown to act out the drama of scholarly life and achievement. At the basketball game, the ten players on the floor become surrogates, acting out on our behalf a conflict in which we shall divide winners from losers, the great from the small, the triumphant from the humiliated. We dress up for weddings, play predictable games at baby showers, and offer toasts to the sister-in-law who's just been promoted at work. In each case, we are using ritual acts to assume roles necessary for the occasion.

Religious rituals are playful as well. They invite us to step into roles otherwise not easily accessible to us, but necessary for our growth toward wholeness. The Lord's Supper is no exception. In this sacrament, the line that divides past from present becomes fuzzy. Past events become, in a sense, present to us. Without leaving our own place and time, we share in the power of past meals that have shaped the identity of Israel and the church.

The earliest written record describing the origins of what we call the Lord's Supper was written by the apostle Paul, near the middle of the first century. He wrote,

> For I received from the Lord what I also handed on to you, that the Lord Jesus on

> the night when he was betrayed took a loaf
> of bread, and when he had given thanks, he
> broke it and said, "This is my body that is
> for you. Do this in remembrance of me."
> In the same way he took the cup also, after
> supper, saying, "This cup is the new
> covenant in my blood. Do this, as often as
> you drink it, in remembrance of me."
>
> (1 Cor. 11:23–25)

Mark's account follows, probably sometime
before A.D. 70, with Matthew and Luke writing
later. Mark and Matthew omit the "remembrance," but Luke reports Jesus' words as "Do
this in remembrance of me," exactly as Paul does.

When we hear the word "remembrance," most
of us are likely to understand it rather differently
than it was originally intended. For us, remembering is basically an action of the mind. We think
of it as taking a psychological journey into the
past. We feel ourselves obligated to create mental
images of an event that occurred a long time ago.
However, the biblical use of the word "remembrance" in relation to the Lord's Supper doesn't
have to do with the effort of trying to imagine a
past event, but with an action: "Do this." The
doing *is* the remembering. It's the action of taking
bread, giving thanks, breaking it, and giving it—
and similar actions with the cup—that serves as
the remembering. Further, the remembering is

something the church does *before God*. It's as though the church were calling out to God, saying, "O God, remember the promises you made in the death and resurrection of your Son!"

Granted, God doesn't have a short memory, and doesn't require that the divine memory be jogged by some reminder from us. It's not a matter of God's having forgotten. This is a different sort of memory held up before God. It's not unlike an occasion when a child might say to a parent, "Remember the time we went on the picnic in the park, and there were geese there, and one of them chased us, and you ran and picked me up and held me, and promised me that it would be OK?" The parent surely would not have forgotten, but the child's recollection becomes a kind of renewal of the experience, bringing into the present moment the feelings of relief and security associated with the event. At the same time, holding up the memory held in common strengthens the bond between parent and child. And so it is that the church holds up this remembrance before God, renewing the bond between God and God's people, and rejoicing in the firmness of the promise made to us in Jesus' death and resurrection.

That this remembering before God was intended to be sealed and reinforced in the context of a meal comes as no surprise. Before, during, and after the time of Jesus, there were established rituals centered on meals all over the Mediterranean basin, including not only Greece and Rome, but also the land of Israel. There were various groups and clubs whose meetings centered on meals that followed prescribed customs and patterns. Some were religious, though most were not. In the case of the Jews, ceremonial meals often resembled meal customs equally familiar to the Greeks and Romans. However, every Jewish meal was understood to be a holy occasion. Whatever the menu may have been, in Jewish meals rituals centering on bread and wine were prominent.

The Lord's Supper as such has its origins in the Last Supper, the meal Jesus shared with his disciples on the Thursday night before his crucifixion on Friday. As Matthew, Mark, and Luke tell the story, it was a Passover meal, although their very brief description of it includes none of the distinctive marks of a Passover meal. The Gospel of John tells the story differently: in his narrative, the meal is not a Passover meal, but a meal eaten the day before Passover. Then, in John's account, Jesus is crucified at the same hour that the Passover lambs were being slain in preparation for the meal to follow that evening.

As far as we can reconstruct the practices of the early Christian church, celebrations of the Lord's Supper did not attempt to replicate a Passover meal. Their practices suggest that what has happened is that Jesus has asked the disciples to continue their meal fellowship after the crisis of his crucifixion, linking his name and identity to the bread and wine they will bless and consume together. Jesus had blessed a loaf of bread and given it to the disciples, saying, "Take; this is my body" (Mark 14:22). Similarly, having blessed the cup, he said, "This is my blood of the covenant, which is poured out for many" (Mark 14:24).

Although its origin lies most specifically in Jesus' *Last* Supper, the *Lord's* Supper is not simply a replay of the *Last* Supper, whether a Passover meal or not. We can presume that people whose names appear in the Bible ate meals on a regular basis, but Scripture mentions only a few such meals. When a meal makes its appearance in Scripture, it's more than just the reporting of a daily occurrence. It points to something significant. When Israel was wandering in the wilderness for forty years, in between the time of bondage in Egypt and arrival in the land of promise, God miraculously provided food. God said to Moses, "I am going to rain bread from heaven for you, and each day the people shall go out and gather enough for that day" (Exod. 16:4). The Gospel of John links this bread to Jesus himself.

> Then Jesus said to them, "Very truly, I tell you, it was not Moses who gave you the bread from heaven, but it is my Father who gives you the true bread from heaven. For the bread of God is that which comes down

from heaven and gives life to the world."
They said to him, "Sir, give us this bread
always."

Jesus said to them, "I am the bread of life.
Whoever comes to me will never be
hungry, and whoever believes in me will
never be thirsty."

(John 6:32–35)

During the same wilderness journey, when
Moses was leading the people ever so slowly to the
promised land, Scripture describes a meal in
which Moses and his brother, Aaron, "came with
all the elders of Israel to eat bread with Moses'
father-in-law in the presence of God" (Exod.
18:12). Later, God invited Moses and a number of
the "elders of Israel" to approach Mount Sinai,
the holy mountain from whose heights God had
spoken. "They beheld God, and they ate and
drank" (Exod. 24:11). These meals, mentioned in
the book of Exodus, are far from routine. They
seal solemn covenants—binding agreements God
has established between God and God's people.
The biblical stories point to meals that are more
than nourishment for the body, but are food for
the soul as well. Key words in these passages may
be "presence" (Exod. 18:12) and "beheld" (Exod.
24:11). God is present in the covenant meal, and
those who eat it discern that presence.

Another meal occasion from the Old Testament occurs when a number of Israelites have come back from their exile in Babylon and begun to rebuild the ruined city of Jerusalem. The book of Nehemiah describes a grand moment in which the returned exiles have gathered in a public place. The scribe Ezra read the book of the law of Moses to the people, and "all the people wept when they heard the words of the law." Then, the religious officials said to the people,

> Go your way, eat the fat and drink sweet wine and send portions of them to those for whom nothing is prepared, for this day is holy. . . . And all the people went their way to eat and drink and to send portions and to make great rejoicing, because they had understood the words that were declared to them.
>
> (Neh. 8:9–10, 12)

This meal is one of rejoicing, because the people understood the law of Moses to be a good gift, and because, having been restored to their own land, it would now be possible to live out that law in ways that had been impossible when they were exiles held captive in a foreign country.

All these Old Testament meals form a background for understanding the meal to which Jesus specifically attached his name and his remembrance. Perhaps "understanding" isn't the best word. The meal Jesus gave to his disciples carries within it the emotional power of bread given to hungry and desperate people in a wilderness; of solemn covenant meals eaten in the presence of God; and of meals of rejoicing among those for whom the long-awaited day of liberation had come.

Although the Lord's Supper receives its primary definition from the Last Supper, it is more than simply a replaying of that final meal Jesus shared with the disciples. The Lord's Supper awakens associations not only with that meal, but also with Old Testament meals, and with meal occasions that occurred during Jesus' ministry. One prominent theme in the Gospels is that Jesus sat at table with "tax collectors and sinners" (Matt. 9:10–11). When the Pharisees criticized him for this, Jesus' response was: "Those who are well have no need of a physician, but those who are sick" (Matt. 9:12). The Lord's Supper recalls these meals, in which Jesus makes himself available to those who have no claim either to purity or to righteousness. Jesus shares the intimacy of table fellowship not to endorse or ignore the sins of his companions, but to be a healing presence.

The stories of Jesus' multiplying the loaves and fish offer particularly striking parallels with the Last Supper narratives. Huge crowds that came out into the country to hear Jesus preach needed to find food when mealtime came around. Jesus directed the disciples to feed the crowd, and they were able to locate five loaves and two fish—hardly enough for more than five thousand people! Jesus had the disciples organize the crowd, and they all sat down.

> *Taking* the five loaves and the two fish, he looked up to heaven, and *blessed* and *broke* the loaves, and *gave* them to the disciples, and the disciples gave them to the crowds. And all ate and were filled.
>
> (Matt. 14:19–20, italics added)

Four verbs occur in this narrative that reappear in the account of the Last Supper: he took, he blessed, he broke, and he gave.

> While they were eating, Jesus *took* a loaf of bread, and after *blessing* it he *broke* it, *gave* it to the disciples, and said, "Take, eat; this is my body."
>
> (Matt. 26:26, italics added)

Whenever we celebrate the Lord's Supper, the miracle of the abundance of food is part of the story that informs our celebration. There is enough, and there will be enough. In the rite, we actively discover that in the taking, blessing, breaking, giving—and in the eating and drinking—there is a place for us at the Table, and a place for our neighbor as well.

Some Questions for Thought

> What sort of "ritual play" have you observed in children? teenagers? adults?

> Are there occasions when, with a parent or grandparent or friend, you bring up the memory of a past event, inviting the person to recall it with you, reliving the fear, anxiety, or delight together?

> Consider meals you have shared with others in the past year. Were there any that served to seal an agreement? solidify a relationship?

> In an uncertain world, where there is no guarantee against scarcity, in what ways might it be true to affirm that "there will be enough"?

CHAPTER 3

TODAY:
EATING AND DRINKING
WITH THE RISEN LORD

Where is Christ when the congregation gathers around the Lord's Table? Is he simply a historical figure, deeply embedded in an ancient time no longer accessible to us? Is he a sacred hero, held captive in the remote reaches of times past, whom we strain to recall with as much vividness as our imaginations might allow? To put it bluntly, is he dead? Or perhaps alive in the highest reaches of heaven, but distant from us?

From early on, Christians have spoken boldly out of their experience at the Lord's Table, insisting that the risen Christ becomes present in their eucharistic celebration. One of the earliest of such testimonies comes from the Gospel of Luke. The Gospel writer tells the story of two members of the larger circle of Jesus' disciples who, on the afternoon of Easter day, were walking to the village of Emmaus, "about seven miles from Jerusalem, and talking with each other about all these things that had happened" (Luke 24:13–14). A stranger joins them. The reader knows that the stranger is Jesus, but the disciples don't recognize him. Jesus joins their conversation, and "beginning with Moses and all the prophets, he interpreted to them the things about himself in all the scriptures" (Luke 24:27). When the three approached Emmaus, the two didn't want to let the stranger go, so they urged him to stay with them. Luke tells us that "when he was at the table with them, he took bread, blessed and broke it, and gave it to them. Then their eyes were opened, and they recognized him" (Luke 24:30–31).

Luke is describing the experience his own church has had at the Lord's Table. As in the narrative of the Last Supper, bread has been taken, blessed, broken, and given, and with the inner eye Jesus' disciples have been enabled to discern his presence among them. This has been the testimony of the larger church down through the centuries: at the Lord's Table, we eat and drink with the risen Lord.

Because we human beings are not very patient with mystery, we like to have explanations for what we have experienced. Over the centuries, pastors and theologians have tried to come up with reasoned arguments to explain and justify our experience at the Lord's Table. Sometimes, in the early centuries, church people would simply say that "something" happened to the bread and the wine, so that it "became" the body and blood of Christ. They were trying to do justice to the profound experience of the people of God at the Lord's Supper, using the language available to them. They weren't arguing a theory about how such a thing might happen.

By the time of Thomas Aquinas, however, in the Middle Ages, theologians felt obliged to produce a sophisticated philosophical argument to support Christian experience. Aquinas borrowed ideas from the philosophy of Aristotle to create a fine-tuned theory about how bread could become Christ's body, and wine become his blood, even though neither appeared to change at all. His explanation became the official doctrine of the Roman Catholic Church. We know it today as the doctrine of transubstantiation.

At the Protestant Reformation in the sixteenth century, all the Reformers took issue with the doctrine of transubstantiation, even when they wanted to affirm the "real presence" of Christ in the Lord's Supper. One of the early reformers, Huldrich Zwingli of Zurich, took the most extreme position, arguing that the bread and wine were no more than reminders of Christ crucified. (Since that explanation is so simple, and so compatible with "modern" sensibilities, it has tended to drive out ways of thinking about the sacrament that require deeper reflection on experience.)

Martin Luther, the first of the reformers, and John Calvin, whose influence has most profoundly shaped Presbyterian developments, were as sure as the Catholics were that Christ becomes present to us in the Lord's Supper, but they disagreed on the details. Luther argued against transubstantiation, but he seemed trapped by the terms of the debate as they had been laid down by the Catholics. Like them, his focus was on "what happened" to the bread and wine. John Calvin, influenced by theologians from very early centuries, didn't accept the terms of debate as framed by the Catholics. His view more nearly resembles that of the Eastern Orthodox churches, who have been less inclined than Roman Catholics to try to describe in minute detail "what happens" to the bread and wine, though no less inclined to affirm the real presence of Christ in the sacrament.

Calvin declined to focus narrowly on the bread and wine alone, doubting that they could be isolated from the whole experience of the Table, including the blessing and consuming of the elements. He believed that Christ became present to the congregation in the entire action of the meal—not excluding the bread and cup, but not limited to them—by the power of the Holy Spirit.

> Now, that sacred partaking of his flesh and blood, by which Christ pours his life into us, as if it penetrated into our bones and

marrow, he also testifies and seals in the Supper—not by presenting a vain and empty sign, but by manifesting there the effectiveness of his Spirit to fulfill what he promises.

(*Institutes of the Christian Religion* 4.17.10)

In the late twentieth century, some Roman Catholic theologians began to sound a good deal like Calvin, introducing the word "transignification" as a better way of speaking about what happens in the sacrament than "transubstantiation." Risking oversimplification, this means that, at a deep level, the Lord's Supper becomes an occasion in which the Spirit changes our perception of the bread and wine, so that we see Jesus Christ in their use, even though there has been no physical change in them.

John Calvin himself had been tempted to overexplain certain of his own doctrines, but in the case of the Lord's Supper, he saw quite clearly that the official Roman Catholic teaching (transubstantiation) was an overexplanation. Based on an authentic kernel rooted in the experience of Christians at the Table, theologians had strained too far to make that experience understandable. Calvin had a good deal to say about the Lord's Supper, but he resisted the temptation to treat it as though contemporary theories about physics could explain the experience.

The key to Calvin's theology of the Lord's Supper, as also in Orthodox theology, is the Holy Spirit. John Knox, Calvin's Scottish admirer, followed his mentor's example. In the Scots Confession, Knox wrote,

> And so we utterly condemn the vanity of those who affirm the sacraments to be nothing else than naked and bare signs. No, we assuredly believe . . . that in the Supper rightly used, Christ Jesus is so joined with us that he becomes the very nourishment and food of our souls. Not that we imagine any transubstantiation of bread into Christ's body, and of wine into his natural blood . . . but this union and conjunction which we have with the body and blood of Christ Jesus in the right use of the sacraments is wrought by means of the Holy Ghost.
>
> (The Scots Confession, chapter 21)

It may come as a surprise to Presbyterians that their church believes as firmly as do the Roman Catholics and the Orthodox and the Lutherans and the Episcopalians that, in the sacrament, we meet the risen Christ, who "becomes the very nourishment and food of our souls." Christ gives himself to us in actions centered on blessing, sharing, and consuming bread and wine. We so believe not based on any theories about how one substance becomes another substance, but based on the same sort of experience known to the early Christians. At the Table, our eyes are opened, and we recognize him (Luke 24:31).

In the early centuries, the church celebrated the Lord's Supper as a feast of great joy, because the dominant theme was that of meeting the risen Lord at the Table. This contrasts strongly with the experience of many today, for whom the Lord's Supper feels like a time of somber reflection on the betrayal and agonizing death of Jesus Christ. Members of one church report that they hear exactly the same music at Communion that they hear at funerals! For several centuries, both Catholics and Protestants approached the Lord's Supper as a kind of funeral for Jesus. It's no wonder that Communion Sundays were best appreciated when only occasional. People needed time between occasions to screw up the courage to face another crucifixion. However, in the latter half of the twentieth century, both Catholics and Protestants began to rediscover the Lord's Suppers of the early church, whose joyful tones had first begun to be obscured and then were lost in the Middle Ages.

Jesus had said, as Paul reports, "For as often as you eat this bread and drink the cup, you proclaim the Lord's death until he comes" (1 Cor. 11:26). In the early centuries, however, it was clear that the crucified Christ could never be separated from the risen Christ. There is sadness in the story of Christ's rejection and death, and there is sadness and loss in our experience of life. Still, the strongest theme of the gospel is that, in the resurrection, God has beaten back the powers of death and hell. The hymn gets it right:

> This is the feast of victory for our God.
>   Alleluia, alleluia, alleluia!
> Worthy is Christ, the Lamb who was slain,
>   whose blood set us free to be people of
>   God.
> Power, riches, wisdom, and strength, and
>   honor, blessing, and glory are His.
> Sing with all the people of God, and join in
>   the hymn of all creation.
> Blessing, honor, glory, and might be to God
>   and the Lamb forever. Amen.
> For the Lamb who was slain has begun His
>   reign. Alleluia!
>   (*The Presbyterian Hymnal*, #594)

When the church celebrates the Lord's Supper, it's not just a matter of turning our eyes around to look back over our shoulders at events of the distant past. We do so in expectation that at each celebration God's self-offering in the death of Christ, and God's triumph in Christ's resurrection, become present and available to us now. The Lord's Supper is not just an exercise in wistful, or painful, nostalgia. It's not the commemoration of a martyred hero, unjustly cut off from the living. The word "celebration" isn't just a figure of speech. The Lord's Supper is indeed a celebration of Jesus Christ, here for us now in solidarity with all our losses; a celebration of the crucified Lord, present beside us in all the cross-shaped places, but also of the risen Lord, trampling down death and bringing good news to the souls in prison (1 Pet. 3:19). It is this same Christ who is our nourishment, our very food and drink. "I am the bread of life. . . . Those who eat my flesh and drink my blood abide in me, and I in them" (John 6:35, 56).

We would do well to consider this when we plan our celebrations of the Lord's Supper. Mournful music and grim demeanor are not really adequate to the occasion. Communion processions and joyful song give sharper focus to the celebratory nature of our festive meal, and honor the Christ who is both our host at the Table and food for our souls.

Some Questions for Thought

> Can you find words to express ways in which Christ has been "present" to you as you shared Holy Communion with others?

> In what ways are members of the congregation "present" to one another?

> What does the hymn mean when it describes the Lord's Supper as a

"feast of victory for our God"?
What kind of "victory"?

What are "cross-shaped places"?
What might it mean to discover
Christ in them?

CHAPTER 4

LOOKING FORWARD: MANIFESTATION OF THE KINGDOM

In the historic Protestant churches, we have largely lost the sense of hopeful expectation that characterized the worship and the faith of the church of the early centuries. In its beginnings, the church was not focused on the past, nor was its interest confined to the present. It leaned toward the future it was confident God was bringing. When the church prayed, "Thy kingdom come," it wasn't a prayer to be uttered distractedly, but a prayer with real force. Nor did they imagine that God's "kingdom" was simply a matter of human progress and gradual improvement. They prayed for God to finish the redemptive work begun in the resurrection of Jesus Christ— to bring into being what the Hebrew prophets described and what the composer Randall Thompson called a "peaceable kingdom." This kingdom is not a kingdom of this world, but one that will heal the brokenness of the world, and transform our tears into joy.

> I will rejoice in Jerusalem,
>   and delight in my people;
> no more shall the sound of weeping be heard
>   in it,
>   or the cry of distress.
> No more shall there be in it
>   an infant that lives but a few days,
>   or an old person who does not live out a
>   lifetime. . . .
> They shall not labor in vain,
>   or bear children for calamity. . . .
> The wolf and the lamb shall feed together,
>   the lion shall eat straw like the ox. . . .
> They shall not hurt or destroy
>   on all my holy mountain.
>   (Isa. 65:19–25)

The words of the prophet Isaiah grope for images that will do justice to the transformation that God has in mind for a "new heaven and a new earth" (Rev. 21:1). It's beyond our imagination. Human language can only hint at what it will be like. The apostle Paul wrote,

> I consider that the sufferings of this present time are not worth comparing with the glory about to be revealed to us. . . . For in hope we were saved. Now hope that is seen

is not hope. For who hopes for what is seen? But if we hope for what we do not see, we wait for it with patience.

(Rom. 8:18, 24–25)

Jesus spoke many times of the coming of the kingdom, and warned his disciples that the transition from our customary daily experience to the day of God's reign might be a wrenching one. When might it be? "But about that day or hour no one knows, neither the angels in heaven, nor the Son, but only the Father. Beware, keep alert; for you do not know when the time will come" (Mark 13:32–33).

During the Middle Ages, the church's hopeful expectation of the reign of God seems to have faded, and interest turned rather more frequently to the past. In modern times, it seems that only fanatics have entertained any interest in the consummation of all things. They have often resorted to attempting to wrench from the Scriptures hidden information about the end times which they link to contemporary events, and at times have even made rather too specific predictions about exactly when God's reign will begin. Because irresponsible interpreters have so frequently hijacked the church's anticipation of God's kingdom, pastors and teachers in the historic churches have reacted by backing away from any mention of such things. A notable exception would be the

Orthodox churches of the East, for whom the coming reign of God has always been the chief focal point of both doctrine and worship.

God's kingdom is not something that human beings can create. Of course, we who are in Christ are animated by our expectation of God's triumphant reign. In Scripture we have a glimpse of what it might look like, so as we engage with our environment we labor to realize in this world something that looks like the kingdom-that-is-to-come. By God's grace, we are sometimes delighted to see signs of the kingdom taking shape among us. Enemies reconcile, peace breaks out where there had been conflict, the strong reach out to the weak, the rich extend a hand to the poor, the hopeless rise up with gladdened hearts. Such signs encourage us, and cause us to thank the God who works miracles. They strengthen our determination to lend our efforts, to the end that other such signs may surface in this broken world. These signs of God's reign renew our hope in the kingdom that is coming, and for which we wait with eager longing.

What does all this have to do with the Lord's Supper? Though the Lord's Supper is rooted in events during Jesus' ministry that are now part of the historical past, and though the Lord's Supper has to do with meeting the risen Lord in the present every time we gather at the Table, it also has to do with God's ultimate future. The Supper itself is a sign of the kingdom that is to come. The apostle Paul wrote, "For as often as you eat this bread and drink the cup, you proclaim the Lord's death *until he comes*" (1 Cor. 11:26, italics added).

The Gospel writers understood the holy Meal as a sign of God's coming reign. The story of the feeding of (at least) five thousand people is a story about the coming kingdom (Matt. 14:13–21; Mark 6:30–44; Luke 9:10–17; John 6:1–13). Whereas Jesus had intended to take the disciples on retreat for a time of rest, crowds of people followed them. Jesus felt compassion for them, for they seemed so badly in need of leadership that cared for their welfare, so he spent the day teaching. Time passed quickly, and it became apparent to the disciples that somebody needed to make some practical arrangements for feeding this huge number of people. Jesus rejected their plan of sending the people away to forage for themselves in nearby villages, and told the disciples, "You give them something to eat." They were dismayed at such a project, but Jesus directed them to find out what supplies might be available in the crowd. They discovered that, in that huge assembly, there were only five loaves and two fish. The disciples brought what they had collected to Jesus, who "looked up to heaven, and blessed and broke the loaves, and gave them to his disciples to set before the people" (Mark 6:41). "And all ate and were filled; and they took up twelve baskets full of broken pieces and of the fish" (vv. 42–43).

It may not be possible to re-create the details of that occasion as a newspaper reporter might like to know them, but the Gospel writers are doing more than simply recording a historical event. They understand the event as a promise. The promise will be kept in the kingdom-that-is-to-come. The Gospel writers are turning the reader's attention toward something that students of the New Testament call the "messianic banquet." In other words, the kingdom of heaven will be like an enormous reunion at which Christ, our Messiah, will be the host. Jesus said, "Then people will come from east and west, from north and south, and will eat in the kingdom of God" (Luke 13:29).

Barbara Brown Taylor has pointed to the sacraments as "road maps to find our way home." In the southern United States, it's not uncommon to read a notice in the newspaper about a country church that's hosting a homecoming, or about a family that's planned a reunion at their home church. The notice often reads, "Dinner on the grounds." The image in my mind is of friends and relatives, cousins and siblings and parents and grandparents and babes in arms gathering from all points of the compass. The license plates may read "North Carolina" or "New York" or "Virginia" or "Kentucky" or even "Ontario." The home folks have provided the meal—ham and fried chicken, potato salad, coleslaw, okra, biscuits, baked beans, corn bread, homemade rolls, and all sorts of pies. It's a feast for the eye as well as for the stomach.

And around the tables there will be storytelling, laughter, and the sharing of wisdom. "Dinner on the grounds" is akin to the Gospel story in which not even a huge number of people exhaust the available resources. In God's kingdom, no one will go without, and there will be plenty for all.

The Lord's Supper is a sort of down payment on the messianic banquet. It has to do with the future at least as much as it has to do with the past and the present. The Lord's Supper is about the kingdom of God. At the holy Table, God sets before our eyes a vision of the table that will be prepared for us in the kingdom. We may discern there the table that resembles the one about which the psalmist sang.

> You prepare a table before me
>   in the presence of my enemies;
> you anoint my head with oil;
>   my cup overflows.
> Surely goodness and mercy shall follow me
>   all the days of my life,
> and I shall dwell in the house of the LORD
>   my whole life long.
>
> (Ps. 23:5–6)

Alexander Schmemann, an Orthodox theologian, has written about the Lord's Supper (Holy Communion or Eucharist) as a "manifestation" of the kingdom. In other words, the Lord's Supper is more than just a vivid symbol of the kingdom-that-is-not-yet. Rather, in the Lord's Supper, God does something. And one of the things God does is to bring the ultimate future into the present, if only for a brief time. This way of looking at the Lord's Supper is entirely consistent with a Reformed, or Presbyterian, understanding of the sacrament. In the holy Meal, people of faith enjoy a foretaste, or down payment, on the table fellowship of the kingdom. We eat and drink with the risen Christ now, as we shall share the feast with him and all the redeemed when the glorious day of consummation has come. Our eyes, then, are turned forward, to the God to whom the ultimate future belongs, "until the day dawns and the morning star rises in [our] hearts" (2 Pet. 1:19).

From as early as New Testament times, the church met weekly on the Lord's day (Sunday, the day of resurrection) to celebrate the Lord's Supper (Acts 2:42 and 20:7). "Lord's day" and "Lord's Supper" went together. Early Christians often spoke of the Lord's day as the "eighth day" of the week, even though technically it was the first of the seven days. They chose this way of speaking because the Lord's day as "eighth day" served as a symbol of eternal life in the kingdom of heaven, after all the other days had been counted out and finished. Sunday (the Lord's day) had a powerful association with the reign of God that was yet to come, just as the Lord's Supper has a similar kinship with the kingdom.

For some centuries, Lord's day and Lord's
Supper were linked, until, in the Middle Ages,
distortions occurred that muted expectation of
the kingdom and associated the Lord's Supper
primarily with the cross alone. Then, although
the priest said the prayers and communed himself every Sunday, ordinary church members did
not go to Communion frequently, if at all. (In
A.D. 1215, church law made it a requirement
that every Christian commune once a year, at
Easter.) At the Reformation, both Luther and
Calvin wanted to restore the ancient church's
practice of both hearing preaching and celebrating the Lord's Supper every Sunday, but civil
authorities stood in the way of Calvin's pro-
gram. Today, Presbyterians have inherited the
practice of a Lord's day service that, more often
than not, does not include the Lord's Supper.

Beginning in the mid-twentieth century, a
number of Presbyterians have begun to move
toward the practice of the early centuries, in
which Lord's day and Lord's Supper go
together—not occasionally, but every week.
Each, in its own way, testifies to the coming
kingdom and nourishes our ardent hope for its
coming. Insofar as the Supper manifests the
kingdom among us, it renews our confidence in
the God whose promise is utterly reliable.

God's project with the human race is to focus
the divine attention not merely on a few human

beings among the many, but on everyone. In Paul's first letter to Timothy, the apostle said,

> For to this end we toil and struggle, because we have our hope set on the living God, who is the Savior of all people, especially of those who believe.
>
> (1 Tim. 4:10)

God's work of redemption is to be worked out not on a small screen, but on a large screen. God's project is to give birth to a new creation. The apostle wrote,

> With all wisdom and insight he has made known to us the mystery of his will, according to his good pleasure that he set forth in Christ, as a plan for the fullness of time, to gather up all things in him, things in heaven and things on earth.
>
> (Eph. 1:8–10)

In the Lord's Supper, we touch base with the deepest reality, which grounds us so that we can live steady and balanced lives in a world of false promises and phantom realities. One of my fondest memories is of a Communion service in the Presbytery of Detroit. We left our seats and formed a Communion procession to receive the bread and cup from several who administered them to us. Standing up and moving toward the

Table, it felt like a pilgrimage toward the kingdom. Seeing the faces around me—black, brown, and white, young and old and in between—provided an intimation of what table fellowship in the kingdom must be like. Standing before those who ministered to us, it was as though we stood at the very doors of the kingdom, waiting to be invited in.

Some Questions for Thought

> The biblical vision of the reign (kingdom) of God stands in sharp contrast to the way things are now. How can paying attention to that contrast affect the way we go about "being church"?

> Have you seen places where it seems that the reign of God has broken out? What did they look like?

> How do you understand Barbara Brown Taylor's suggestion that the sacraments (in this case, the Lord's Supper) function as "road maps to find our way home"?

> What does it look like when you think of the Lord's Supper as something that God does rather than something we do?

CHAPTER 5

THE GREAT THANKSGIVING

At a Communion service hosted by another denomination, it was evident that there was bread and grape juice on the Table, but no one quoted Scripture, prayed over loaf and cup, or even touched them until the servers came forward. Instead of prayer, the presiding minister made a few sermonic observations about the cross, presuming that everyone in the congregation knew what the Lord's Supper was about, just needing to be exhorted a little bit to be duly appreciative of Jesus' agony and death for our sakes.

In Presbyterian congregations, worshipers will always hear the Words of Institution (quotes from the scriptural accounts of Jesus' directing his disciples to "do this" in remembrance of him), and almost always be led in some sort of prayer over the loaf and cup. But what sort of prayer?

Every New Testament account of Jesus' insti-
tuting the Lord's Supper includes versions of the
same sequence of verbs—took, gave thanks,
broke, and gave. (When these verbs are used in
the same sequence elsewhere, they are meant
to draw our attention so that we make a connec-
tion with the Lord's Supper. For example, in the
stories of the feeding of the multitudes, or in the
story of the meal at Emmaus.) While no New
Testament account goes into detail about exactly
what this taking, thanking, breaking, and giving
looked like in practice, the consistent use of such
verbs seems to tell us that, from the beginning,
the Lord's Supper had some sort of generally
predictable form. In all probability, actual practice varied from community to community, and
from place to place. Nevertheless, there was at
least a minimal structure.

We know that whenever a group gathered for
a special meal in the ancient world, they followed
forms that had the force of ritual. This isn't alto-
gether different from hospitality at meals today,
even in our informal society. When dinner
guests arrive at a home in our neighborhood, the
hosts greet them at the door, show them in (or
out to a patio or deck), offer them something to
drink or an appetizer, make conversation, then
proceed to the meal, followed by more conversation and then leave-taking. There are other
ways to conceive of hosting a dinner party, but

this form, however casually it may be observed, is familiar ritual. In Jesus' time, Jewish dinner parties were holy occasions, and they proceeded according to rituals known to everyone.

It is reasonable to imagine that at meals Jesus shared with his disciples (including the last one), they proceeded according to familiar norms. The meal might begin with a ritual hand washing. Each arriving guest would be given a cup of wine. The guest would drink it, repeating a blessing over the wine. The meal would officially begin when the host broke bread and offered a blessing. Various courses and cups of wine would follow, with appropriate blessings. When the meal reached an end, there was another hand washing, and then followed the chief prayer of the meal, recited over the last cup of wine—the "cup of blessing" (1 Cor. 10:16).

Although in American society we value informality and spontaneity, it would be a mistake to imagine that these were values in New Testament times, or, indeed, would be in most of the world even today. Even in our own case, more often than we imagine, informality and spontaneity are constrained by hidden norms. It is more difficult to imagine Jesus and the disciples—or anyone in the first century—sharing a meal without prayers and blessings than with formal prayers and blessings.

Jewish and Gentile churches may have developed different patterns from each other and

from whatever patterns were most familiar to
Jesus and the Twelve, but their celebrations of
the Lord's Supper certainly were not formless.
Around A.D. 150, a man named Justin Martyr,
writing from Rome, offered one of the earliest
descriptions of Christian worship. Even then, he
didn't offer much detail, but he says that, when
the assembly gathers for worship on the Lord's
day, the "president of the brethren"

> sends up praise and glory to the Father of
> all, through the name of the Son and Holy
> Spirit, and offers thanksgiving at some
> length . . . When he has finished the prayers
> and the thanksgiving, all the people present
> shout their assent, saying, "Amen."

> *(First Apology)*

So, at this early date, we know this much about
how they were celebrating the Lord's Supper in
Rome, at least. A presiding officer prayed over
the bread and cup. The prayer had a Trinitarian
reference (even though the doctrine of the Trinity as such would not be officially formulated for
another two hundred years). It had the tone of
praise and thanksgiving. The presiding officer
was praying on behalf of all those assembled,
who affirmed the prayer and made it their own
with a bold "Amen."

For the next two or three centuries, scattered
churches that had developed separately became

acquainted with one another by way of travelers and exchanges of visits, and common practices of celebrating the Lord's Supper began to emerge. Particularly in the churches of the East, prayer at the Table became more and more clearly Trinitarian, with a strong theme of thanksgiving, and included prayer for the Holy Spirit to manifest the risen Christ in the Meal.

In churches of our own time, at celebrations of the Lord's Supper one looks for some resemblance to the taking, blessing, breaking, and giving familiar from the New Testament accounts and the early centuries of the church. While the Lord's Supper may not look exactly the same in every congregation, there ought to be a certain recognizable structure, at least in the historic denominations. The "taking" of bread and cup, whether they are brought to the Communion Table at the offering, or have simply been placed there before the service began, is well-nigh universal. In most Presbyterian congregations, the presiding minister breaks the bread, certainly an important part of the ancient structural sequence, and in every case the bread and cup will be given to the people. The uncertainty often arises at the point of "blessing," or "giving thanks."

The New Testament uses both these words in its Meal stories. Matthew and Mark use "give thanks," while Luke and Paul (First Corinthians) use "bless." The two words are not far apart. In Hebrew, the word for "bless" can also mean to give thanks and praise. Neither in Jewish practice nor in Christian practice as it took form in the early churches was "blessing" or "giving thanks" a minimal sort of affair, a hurried grace before meals. Nor was such prayer somber and gloomy, a sort of lamentation for the tragedy of the cross. Nor was it an exhortation to people of faith to transport themselves back to Good Friday, to summon up an appropriately sober reflection on Jesus' sacrifice. Prayer at the Table, from as early as we know, was doxological, which is to say it resembled a great song of praise and thanksgiving. This, then, is the sort of prayer over the Meal that we ought to expect in church today.

In the last century or so, both Catholics and Protestants have begun to pay careful attention to patterns of praying at the Lord's Table as they developed historically. The result has been that all the historic churches have begun to honor a pattern of celebration that is remarkably similar. For Roman Catholics, Vatican Council II led to a significant departure from their tradition of eucharistic prayer. Protestants, too, have reexamined inherited traditions and found them less than fully adequate. As the historic churches have developed new services and service books, they have reached a surprising consensus. It's not a case of Catholics imitating Protestants, or vice versa, but rather a case of each rediscovering treasures lost centuries ago. Serendipitously, we are laying claim to these treasures which, after all, belong to us all equally.

Our Presbyterian Directory for Worship (part of the church's Constitution) has laid out a description of the ancient and newly recovered form of prayer at the Lord's Table. The denomination's *Book of Common Worship* provides a similar description, as well as many full texts for such prayers. In the *Book of Common Worship*, prayer at the Lord's Table is called the Great Thanksgiving, an appropriate name for this prayer of thankful praise.

The prayer, like prayers from the Eastern churches of early centuries and like the creeds (for example, the Apostles' Creed and the Nicene Creed), has a Trinitarian form. The first section offers praise and thanks to God for creating the world; for God's work of redemption, especially in the history of Israel; and for, at last, sending Jesus Christ. From ancient times, this first section concluded with the assembled congregation's sung praise, usually from a version of Isaiah 6 or Revelation 4: "Holy, holy, holy Lord, God of power and might . . . ," and concluded, "Blessed is he who comes in the name of the Lord" (Ps. 118:26 and John 12:13).

The second section of the Great Thanksgiving focuses specifically on God's mighty acts in

Jesus Christ: his incarnation, holy life, death, burial, resurrection, ascension, and promise of coming again. Often, the congregation also sings an acclamation after this section, such as "Christ has died, Christ is risen, Christ will come again."

The third section of the prayer, of deep significance to all Christians but especially to those who trace their history from John Calvin, is a prayer for God to send the Holy Spirit upon us and upon the gifts of bread and wine. It is unimaginable that Presbyterians would neglect this part of the prayer, since, as Calvin taught, it is only by the action of the Spirit that Christ becomes present to and for us in the Meal.

The Great Thanksgiving ends with a grand doxology to the Holy Trinity. "Through Christ, with Christ, in Christ, in the unity of the Holy Spirit, all glory and honor are yours, almighty Father, now and forever." After which, as in Justin Martyr's description from the second century, all sing or say boldly, "Amen!"

The Great Thanksgiving praises God, gives thanks, and asks God to make us one with Christ and one another, and to form us as the body of Christ in service to the world. It rehearses the great and essential themes of the gospel much as the creeds do. The prayer is rooted in the past—specifically, in biblical history—and turns us toward the future—the coming kingdom, in which our hope lies—and rejoices in the gift of

Christ's own self in the present. To pray this prayer regularly—whether in the exact words of provided texts or in words of the presiding minister's own devising—is to rehearse and absorb into one's soul what the gospel is all about. Whoever wanders into a Presbyterian congregation, puzzled about what's happening at that Table, may grow into an acquaintance with its faith by listening attentively to this glorious Thanksgiving.

Some Questions for Thought

In Jewish prayer, thanking God often involved telling a story—particularly, a story about God's gracious works among God's people. If you were to thank God by telling a story, what would the story be?

There are various postures for prayer. Sometimes people kneel, sometimes they sit with bowed heads, sometimes eyes are closed and sometimes open, sometimes people stand and raise their hands and faces. Which postures most clearly signal or encourage praise and thanksgiving?

Christians often sing sections of the Great Prayer of Thanksgiving at the Table. They sing "Holy, holy, holy Lord . . ." and "Blessed is he who comes in the name of the Lord," and "Christ has died, Christ is risen, Christ will come again," and they may sing the Great "Amen" that concludes the prayer. How is singing something different from saying it, or hearing someone else say it? In what ways might singing parts of this corporate prayer engage the congregation in it?